Spiritual MIND

VICTOR L. BRACKETT JR.

ISBN 979-8-88616-251-6 (paperback)
ISBN 979-8-88616-252-3 (digital)

Christian Faith Publishing
832 Park Avenue
Meadville, PA 16335
www.christianfaithpublishing.com

Printed in the United States of America

I would like to dedicate this inspirational book to three of most extraordinary spiritual women that I have ever known that really inspired me to be great.

First, I want to thank my deceased mother, Minister Delotha Brackett Rogers, for the encouragement that she provided me and always challenging me to do what was righteous in the eyes of God. She also taught me to never give up on the dream that God put down in my heart and really helped me to acknowledge that with God, all things are possible if I only just believe.

I also would like to thank my deceased grandmother, Overseer Chanie Holloway, for being my spiritual advisor and always praying God's blessing upon my life. I also want to give her the credit for helping me to acknowledge my true calling and gift. Overseer encouraged me to embrace my calling by listening to the words that God was saying to me and writing them down verbatim.

Lastly, but certainly not least, I want to thank my beautiful wife, Beverly Thomas Brackett. She is a phenomenal woman. Besides being my life partner for over twenty-five years, she has helped me raise our three loving children. Victor lll, Vonte, and Victoria. And she is a wonderful mother to them all. She also really keeps me grounded in my flesh while always elevating me in my spirit and really understands God's purpose for my life.

May God forever pour out his blessings on each of these magnificent women in life, as well as in death.

Christian Call

One day, I got a phone call from Sister Marie. She was a Christian of faith who wanted to publish me. She said, "I listened to your words, and they really sounded nice. Will you mind writing your words down in God's book of life?" Even though I just spoke to my sister on the phone, it was something in her tone that made me feel at home.

Sister Marie didn't know me, and she never saw my face. But it was something in her voice that said mercy and grace. She really believed in me and showed blind faith. She told me, "All your dreams can all come true if you just trust in the Lord and just see it through. God can do great and marvelous things through you. Your words are powerful, and you can really bless someone because the power of life and death is in the power of your tongue."

"Oh, Sister Marie," I said, "I must confess. I really couldn't have testimony if I didn't have a test."

She said, "Oh, yes, my brother, please don't stress because there is no message if you didn't have a mess."

I said, "Hey, Sister Marie, what a powerful thing to say. You're such a blessing, my sister. You spoke the words of the day. These words were quiet, but they spoke loud in truth. My spirit was lifted, and my faith was renewed. Now, I can raise my head high, and I can stand up tall. God bless you, Sister Marie. Thank you for the call."

Inspirational Quote

"God don't give us all wisdom, because we all don't use common sense. Until we use common sense, we have no use for wisdom."…

Victor L. Brackett Jr.

Inspirational Quote

"Mind you, it's good to imagine and wonder, but wonder and imagine what would you do with a good mind."…

Victor L. Brackett Jr.

Inspirational Quote

"In the silence of darkness, God still sees
your sadness and hears your hurt."…

Victor L. Brackett Jr.

Inspirational Quote

"People can change your destination, but they can't change your destiny; because your destination is your place, but your destiny is your purpose."…

Victor L. Brackett Jr.

Inspirational Quote

"The real foundation of a home is not defined on how it's built from the outside, but how it's built from the inside."…

Victor L. Brackett Jr.

Inspirational Quote

"Small rocks are hard to move on the surface in a river flood, but large rocks are harder to move when submerged under the sea."...

Victor L. Brackett Jr.

Inspirational Quote

"When the world is the darkest, the stars in heaven shine the brightest."…

Victor L. Brackett Jr.

Inspirational Quote

"It's much easier to sleep with a heavy heart than a heavy mind; with sleep your heart will find rest, but your mind will continue to wonder."…

Victor L. Brackett Jr.

Inspirational Quote

"It's better to give constructive criticism than to receive destructive criticism; because genuine constructive criticism will build you up, but destructive criticism will tear you down."…

Victor L. Brackett Jr.

Inspirational Quote

"The right words can build up one's confidence, but with the wrong words, one's confidence can be torn down."…

Victor L. Brackett Jr.

My Beautiful Butterfly

When I close my eyes and open my hands,
my beautiful butterfly filters like sand.

My butterfly wings are fragile and yet so strong.
I open my eyes, and my butterfly was gone.

Where can my beautiful butterfly be?
There she is, floating across the sea.

My butterfly is light and stings like a black widow.
And still she is harmless and gentle as a caterpillar.

Now my caterpillar is flying high in the sky.
Fly, my butterfly, my beautiful butterfly, just fly.

I pray my butterfly's wings take her very far.
And still I'm optimistic and I leave an open jar.

Where can my beautiful butterfly be?
There she is, floating across the sea.

Dear God

Dear God,

My mama was buried in an unmarked plot, just in case you forgot. Bless me now my Savior, and forget me not. And still, I refuse to believe that you are cruel to me. For henceforth and forevermore, you said you'll bless her seed.

I'm standing here in awe of you, contemplating my thoughts, trying hard not to be bitter, but I'm seasoned with salt but so glad that I was baptized and washed in the blood of the Lamb. I was scandalized and criticized by "fam."

They said that I was nothing, but still, I am who you say I am. So I am realizing and finalizing the death that you dealt, but I know well indeed whence comes my help. So I keep waiting and praying for your beloved Son. I know the darkest hour is just before dawn.

The selfishness of me wanted Mama to stay, but God, thank you for evening my pain and taking hers away.

If it got to be, so let it be, so "sleep, Mama, sleep," at least her tears won't be so bitter and their taste so sweet. God, I hear the questions that you are asking me, "Would my sadness suffocate me so I can't breathe?" Or "Would it compel me to my destiny?" I know this would only make me better. I know you still love me. That's why I wrote you this letter.

Mama spent all her life preaching and teaching about the promised land, but Mama never could've wrote this lesson plan.

So I wish her safe travels on her holy caravan, where the sun has set over the ocean that cools the burning sands. And on her travel, if her feet get tired, why don't you swing down your chariot Lord? And let sweet low ride. So, God, I will finish this letter by asking you just to keep holding my hand. I won't end this letter with "yours truly." I will only just say, "Amen."

My Piano

Through my sweet piano sounds of a long glistening night, there are thirty-six black keys and fifty-two white. There is love, peace, and harmony that fill the world with delight; the sounds of my piano when my soul wants peace; and eighty-eight keys that can tame a savage beast.

My piano plays for blessing that comes from above. It plays just to share God's inseparable love. My piano crises for "salvation," and it screams, "He reins," just as so soft as a pillow and clear as a windowpane. My piano has no month, and yet it can speak. It tells me when to wake up and tells me when to sleep.

My piano can speak loud, and yet it can whisper with such smooth and soothing sounds that can make you shiver.

My piano is so soft, so gentle, so meek; it says, "Hallelujah," whenever it speaks.

My piano often speaks and tells many stories while demonstrating God's splendor and magnificent glory.

My piano whispers, "Lord, I want to thank you just for another day, just for waking me up and starting me on my way. As I rise and shine and wash my face, I like to thank you Lord, for your amazing grace. I like to thank you Lord, with morning worship and praise."

Thirty-six black keys and fifty-two white create peace and harmony that fill the world with delight.

Angel of Mercy

When I open my eyes, what do I see? It's my angel of mercy
that stands beside me. White hat, white dress, and white shoes,
I seen. She wears a white cape that spreads like wings.
She tells me what to do and holds my hand while gently
giving me a bedpan. She gives me medicine when I cough;
while she adjusts her red cross. She gives me water to clear
my throat, then she helps me put on my bath coat.

I really don't know where I'd be without my beautiful
Angel of mercy. She gives me love with lots of care;
while she says a little prayer…

"Lord, I know you are the master of all and Father
I know you know best; but if you decide to take my patients,
I just ask that you give them rest. Lord, you know I'm
just a nurse, and I'm here to do your will; but if
I ask in Jesus's name, I know you are able to heal.
Lord, I know you died on the cross for all humanity's sins."
She thanked the Father just for listening; then politely said…
"Amen."

Tuck in my pillow, pull up my covers, and take my
temperature now; with my angel of mercy by my side,
I know I can make it somehow.

My Unseen God

Close your eyes and imagine me,
My unseen God I can't see.

I often wonder where can he be,
My unseen God that created me.

He left his footprints across the sea,
But still, I wonder where can he be.

I can hear his voice in the air,
I turned around, and he's not there.

I wonder where can he be,
My unseen God that I can't see.

I search the stars and moon;
I even search his empty tomb.

I wonder where can he be,
My unseen God that looks like…
Me.

Fish and Bread

I'd like to tell you a miracle that you never knew,
what Jesus did, what they said he couldn't do.
Now, this is what I heard, and this is what they said,
how he fed five thousand with five loaves of bread.

I wish I had been there and had my dish,
When he fed five thousand with two little fish.
He told his disciples what they should know;
"Sit them down!" he said, and they did as he said so.

Jesus took the fish, and he took the bread; he gave
thanks to the Father, and five thousand were fed.
I wish I had been there and had my dish,
when Jesus fed them with bread and fish.

I wish I had been there when they were fed,
by two little fish and five loaves of bread.
Was it for real or just a dream when they witnessed
this miraculous thing? I can imagine what they said
when Jesus fed them with fish and bread.

The more and more they got fed, down came more and more
bread. The more and more they got fill, up came
more and more fish gills. I can imagine what they
said when Jesus fed them with fish and bread.

The Holloway Road

A long, long time ago, a man walked a narrow road.
He was a good man; I was told. There is a shining
light that shines day and night on this road.
I was told that this road is very old. The name of this
road is called the Holloway Road. People say that when you
walk this long road, you find love and peace, I've been told.
They say that this road is paved with gold; God has built the
narrow road. One day, the man was walking up this road.
He met a beautiful woman, I've been told. He said,
"Hello, my name is Morris." She said, "God sent me
by this way. My name is Chanie, I'll walk with you along
the way." Soon, there were little footsteps behind them
on this road. God said, "He will watch over them rather
it be her or him on this Holloway Road." They walked this
road together for many years. There was laughter; sometimes,
there were tears, but yet God was with them throughout
the years. Then one day, the man said to his wife, "I'm getting
tired. I'm going to walk over to the other side." She said,
"I will see you again. I'll keep walking with Jesus until this
road comes to the end." One day, I started walking on this same
Holloway Road. I know God is walking beside me on that
same Holloway Road. You know that road, that road that
is paved with gold.

Heavenly Prayer

Oh, heavenly Father, I pray to you, so wise and gentle and
    strong.
Heavenly Father, I pray to you that guides this sinner from
    wrong.

Oh, heavenly Father, I pray to you, so mild, so humble, and
    meek.
Heavenly Father, I pray to you that rocks my soul to sleep.

Oh, heavenly Father, I pray to you that created the stars and
    moon.
Heavenly Father, I pray to you, that makes the flowers bloom.

Oh, heavenly Father, I pray to you, who created the winds
    and sea.
Heavenly Father, I pray to you who can save a sinner like me.

Oh, heavenly Father, I pray to you, who shows us wonders
    and signs.
Heavenly Father, I pray to you, who can turn water into wine.

Oh, heavenly Father, I pray to you, who ten thousand souls
    you fed.
Heavenly Father, I pray to you, who can turn stone into head.

Oh, heavenly Father, I pray to you, that created the heaven
    and earth.
Heavenly Father, I pray to you that declared me free from
    birth.

Oh, heavenly Father, I pray to you, who is the Prince of Peace.
Heavenly Father, I pray to you who's holy face I seek.

Oh, heavenly Father, I pray to you, that precious name I love.
Heavenly Father, I pray to you that sends his glory from
    above.

Oh, heavenly Father, I pray to you, who died on a wooden
    cross.
Heavenly Father, I pray to you who paid this sinner's cost.

Rain Comes Down

Rain comes down from far, far above.
Rain comes down, like a gentle white dove.

Rain comes down so soft and so sweet.
Rain comes down in likeness of a sheep.

Rain comes down, in great numbers you can't tally.
Rain comes down, like lilies in the valley.

Rain comes down from above and so far.
Rain comes down, like a bright morning star.

Rain comes down, like waves in the sea.
Rain comes down, like a smoke burning tree.

Rain comes down, like grains of gritty sand.
Rain comes down in likeness of a man.

Rain comes down, with lighting and thunder.
Rain comes down so meek and so humble.

Rain comes down, like loud horns in Zion.
Rain comes down in likeness of a lion.

Rain comes down, like many straws in a broom.
Rain comes down, like a handsome bridegroom.

Rain comes down before the beginning.
Rain comes down after the ending.

Twelve Steps to Salvation

Step one: Raise the dead.

Step two: Turn stone into bread.

Step three: Turn water into wine.

Step four: Heal the blind.

Step five: Make the lame walk.

Step six: Make the dumb talk.

Step seven: Give eternal life.

Step eight: Be a sacrifice.

Step nine: Save the lost.

Step ten: Die on the cross.

Step eleven: Be buried in a grave.

Step twelve: Rise in three days.

4 Eternal Life

There once was a man that had a plan to die on a wooden
cross.
4 if he didn't die and pass us bye, all the world will be lost.

4 the day he died, his mother cried and keeled at the man's
feet.
4 many were sad, but few were glad and grateful 4 one lost
sheep.

Although he was innocent and did no wrong, he died with
two dirty crooks.
4 one was doomed 4 a dead man's tomb and another was let
off the hook.

4 he told his mother and his brothers that he was going to
visit his dad;
4 it really didn't matter to his mother, she still was very sad.

4 then she remembered what the man said, 4 it really wasn't
the end.
4 it was not where his life had stop; it was where his life had
begin.

Heavenly Dream

I often dream about a place such as this,
Where God's saints can come and
Just reminisce about the time of struggles
And pains of old life.

No more tears, no more fears, no more worries,
And no more strife.
I feel the wind beneath my feet,
Oh, Lord, is this the heaven that I seek?
The safe haven for the meek.

I pray I lived a beautiful life,
If I opened my eyes, would it be paradise?
Living the dream so long foretold,
Talking to the saints of old and
walking on the streets of gold.

I see *Elijah in his chariot of fire!*
Would he take me to my King and Sire?
So I can look upon his face and worship his holy grace.
Oh, what a wonderful sight,
to see Seven thousand angels at flight!
Pretty white doves cover the skies, and the sun always rise,
And darkness never fills the night,

Because it's always eternal light.
The most beautiful flowers I ever
seen, please don't wake me,
Just let me dream.

Lord, before you laid me down to sleep,
I prayed to you my soul you'll keep.
And if I die before I awake, I pray it's here my soul you take.
Have you ever been anywhere that felt so real,
When nothing was the essence and time stood still?

Can you imagine a place without sin,
When everyone you meet is your friend?
It may be hard to believe, but you have no enemies.
For here, there is no use for money,
There are rivers flowing with milk and honey.

Here, there is no mortgage or rent,
You have mansions that are magnificent.
For there are many rooms, with windows and boards,
Lots of land but only one Lord.
There are tables of food with heavenly wines,
There are fruits with heavenly vines,
Angels singing in unity, "God our Father,
"We adore thee, in this holy city of Trinity.
"Oh, what a glorious place to be,
"Please don't wake me; just let me sleep."

Sing, Child!

When you wake up in the morning to the glorious sun
and the weight of the world feels like a ton.
(Sing child)

When you have no clothes and no shoes for your feet,
your rent is due, and you have nothing to eat.
(Sing child sing)

When the friends you lost and thought you had
left you alone, disheartened, and sad.
(Sing child)

When your eyes are full of tears and you are feeling so blue
and that old devil laughs and says, "Jesus doesn't love you."
(Sing child sing)

When you prayed to God seemly with your last breath
and you gave to the Lord until there was nothing left.
(Sing child)

When that spouse you trusted broke your marriage vow,
left you shaking your head and wondering,
Heavenly Father, how?
(Sing child)

When that child you raised in the church and upright
now serving hard times, twenty-five to life.
(Sing child, sing).

But you know that God is always good;
now, everything is better.
Now, that weight of the world feels light as a feather.

Now he's blessed me with clothes and plenty of shoes.
The rent is paid up and in advance too!

My so-called friends weren't friends indeed, but that's okay,
Because Jesus was the friend I really needed.

God has taken his hand and wiped my tears.
Now, I'm no longer blue and have nothing to fear.

The power I got; it came from up above;
now, Satan truly knows that
"Jesus is love!"

The trust is restored in my married life, because
Jesus said, "I can be your husband, or I can be your wife."

The child I thought I lost and would only see in a grave,
only serve three years and got out on good behavior.

When I think about Jesus and the goodness of these things.
(Sing child, sing child, sing child, sing!)

Saint Chanie

She came from the hills of Kentucky; *vigorous, beautiful,* and *young.* She married one husband and had nine children, five daughters and four sons. She's *great grandmother* to some, *grandmother* to most, and *mother* to many that we all can boast. Never letting nature get the last say, we watched her age for many years, but we watched her age with grace.

She often shares her canny wisdom with her daughters and her sons, teaching what she knew the most; Jesus, Abraham, Peter, and John. "Listen, my children," she said. "Listen to what I say. When all else fails and doesn't go well, you can always pray. For the lessons I teach are very deep, they go deeper than a bottomless well. For drink my children, and thirst no more, or drink from a bottomless *hell.*

One day, *Chanie* got sick and just could not get well. Old death paid her a visit, for this was an invitation death could not turn down and certainly would not resist because all he wanted and he wished was just for one foul and fatal kiss.

But *God* stretched out his mighty hands, and in a loud voice, he spoke, "Dry up you cancerous bones," and suddenly, *Chanie* awoke. "Get back, death," he commanded. "She has my work to do. Build me a mission. Don't be afraid, for lo *Chanie,* I am always with you. The power of life and death is in your tongue, so always be mindful of what you say. Complete this task, and stay steadfast, and they will call you *Saint Chanie* one day."

So for years, she preached, and faithfully, she teached, and her power stayed so real. So *God* said, "Rest for a while. Watch over my sheep." So he ordained her his *overseer*. So *Chanie* did what she was told and looked over the Master's sheep.

With eyes like an eagle, she watched, and she prayed with a keen beak. She watched over the flock by day, and she watched over the flock by night. Even when she closed her eyes to sleep, the sheep were still in sight. So this is a story about *Chanie*, a *Saint* she just happens to be. If she stays steadfast and completes her task, then one day, they will call her *Saint Chanie*.

Preach the Word!

Preach the Word is what I heard! Time, time, and again.
But oh my *Lord*, it's so hard to preach when you're so deep
in iniquity and sin. I try to open my mouth to shout,
but no words come out. My head is like lead because it's
heavy with truth, full of numbers, scriptures, and chapters,
like that great "Book of Ruth."

But where will I go, what would I say are the questions when
I pray. But I know if I go, *Hosanna* will lead the way.
Since I was a little buck to a woodchuck, you see I was born
in this life, and the only way out will be the ultimate sacrifice.
And even then, my friend, I'll live this eternal life.
Victor is my name, and no, I'm not ashamed; you got
V-I-C-T-O-R! And yes, you can ask me why.

Because *victory* is what I got when *Jesus* hung
his head, bleed, and died. I was blinded like Saul and
couldn't see how someone like him can love someone like me.
But like Saul, I was change to Paul, and now, I'm a new creature,
maybe I'm "poet" or maybe I am a "preacher."

The more I talk and the more I speak, the little voice in my head
is screaming, "That's right; preach! Preach!" Like my
Lord Jesus Christ, I came to serve, so take a seat.
I'm going to wash your feet; then I'm going to feed you the Word.
Because the spirit of the *Lord* is upon me, and I can fill his

presence for sure; he has anointed me to preach the gospel
and spread good news to the poor.

He has sent me to heal the brokenhearted, and preach the
      captives free.
And whosoever the Son set free is truly free indeed.
Because man cannot live on bread alone, neither chicken, or rice,
nor gravy and neck bones. Not the kind of food that we eat
in the south but the kind of food that proceeds out of *God's*
mouth. I'll have another taste if I could (umh, umh, umh).

Now, you taste and see if the *Lord* is good. I didn't come to
showboat; I didn't come to entertain, but I did come to let you
know that *Jesus Christ* still reigns. I'm going to open up my
mouth and preach, and I'm going to let the *Lord* deliver.
So listen to the words I speak as they flow like the Jordan River.

I wonder how "John the Baptist" stayed focus, while he preached
in the wilderness, eating wild honey and locus.
No congregation and nobody to see, but "the Baptist" still
      preached
repent to the cactus trees. Now, that's the kind of preacher I
want to be; wait a minute; let me thank my "Grandma Chanie"
for praying for me. So did my momma, my uncles, and all
      my aunties.

For I know that they prayed for me with their hearts and
      their souls,
because we all walk this "Holloway Road." Just a little while
longer y'all, I'm almost through, but like *Jesus* said,
"I am the living truth." Now, may the *Lord* watch between
me and you, until you see me and I see you; now, you pray
for me my sisters and my brothers while we are absent, one
from another.

Radio

Turn on the radio, and listen; now, you tell
me this world don't need fixing.

A little boy shot his mother with a gun.
They ask the kid, "Why?" His only reply,
"I only just did it for fun."

A baby was found the other day, wrapped
up in the trash can around the way.

It seems like the whole world is so mean.
Today, a drug dealer stabbed a crack fiend.

O' Lord, when will this madness end?
But still, I turn on the radio and listen.

We can't seem to keep the hungry fed,
Because another homeless man was found dead.

Cain killed Abel for a beeper; he replied,
"Was I my brother's keeper?"

The devil's roaring to and fro,
But still, I turn on the radio.

It's five dollars a pound for market meat,
and still y'all, it's a recall on beef.

Gasoline at an all-time high, some people
Still rather walk then fly.
(News flash!)
"Another church set on fire!"

O God, please! help our poor souls,
But still, Lord, I turn on the radio!

Adam is divorcing Eve to marry Steve.
Lord, that's just a shame! Each and every
Day, I pray; I ask, "Why so much pain?"

The board of education is breaking the rules,
screaming! "Just say no kids, to prayer in schools."

The radio said, "The preachers are lunatics!"
Because they're preaching about politics.

O' Lord, for heaven's sake! You can't
Separate the church from state.

Democrats and Republicans are keeping up fuss.
And they say, "One nation under
God, and in God, we trust."

O' Lord, "I just can't listen any mo'!"
was the words that I echoed.
But still Lord, I turn on the radio!

Hell with Jezebel!

I was in the pulpit one Sunday morning, and that's where I
seen her. Lord, she had shapes and curves, and she was
fast like Talladega. When she sees me, she greets me,
with a kiss, huge, and smile. That's the kind of love
and affection that drives a good preacher wild.

In the name of "Jesus!" I tried to rebuke, but how do you
bind a woman so seductive and loose? Oh, Lord, please help
me because I'm in a mess, with bone of my bone and
flesh of my flesh. I'm in a love triangle between me, God,
and a dress. The devil is a liar, and her temptation is strong.
She said, "To love you is right; not to love me is wrong."

My spirit is willing, but my body is so weak, now no power
in the midnight hour, and I sleep so deep, laid up in a hot bed,
in hell fiery sheets, with the most beautiful thing I ever seen
and the sweetest thing I smelled. She said, "Hello you, it was
nice to know you; my name is Jezebel."

Now, Jezebel is very sweet, and she might just taste like honey.
But please believe; she will deceive; she's very crafty and
cunning. Her ambition is to detour your mission and ministry
she will deploy. She sits and dreams how she can scheme
to seek, devour, and destroy!

I can't seem to help myself; Jezebel makes it so hard.
But with a kiss, I reminisce that I'm in love with
a jealous God. So I went down on my knees, and I cried,
"Please forgive me, my beautiful precious Lord so let be!
"Create in me a clean heart you can see, and renew a
"right spirit within me."

Now, I'm committed to my Lord, with a new dedication.
Because I know my God has forgiven me, for my lust
and fornication. If you listen, live, and learn, then this
lesson you can't fail. If you won't believe and don't conceive,
then it's "hell with Jezebel!"

Praying Dead Hands

Lay your dead hands on me *Chanie*, one *more time*,
so your sweet Holy Ghost Spirit can bless mine.

From the *crown of my head* to the soul of my feet,
May God forgive me for disturbing your sleep.

As your body lay down *cold in suspense*, I kneel down
for my sweet and *farewell kiss*. I know you can't hear
me and you can't *speak* because old death finally kissed
your left cheek.

As you lay in silence with your hands fold,
I *pray* God blesses your *Holy Ghost* soul.

You told me to eat and I ate, but this was
so *hard to swallow*; but still, I thank God
for the footsteps you left on the road that
I must follow.

I got *ninety-one tears* for *ninety-one years* that you live.
But still Lord, I can't help the way I *feel*. So I *mourn*

and I *cry all the night through*, but the *tears* I cry
are not for you; they are for me and yours that you
left behind, so *faithfully* we wait for your *sweet holy sign*.

So *lay your dead hands on me*, Chanie, one more time,
So your sweet Holy Ghost Spirit can bless mine.

For *sure* we know that weeping may endure for a night,
my God warned me; but still I know that this joy I
have will cometh in the morning.

This was like plucking a flower out of weeds.
God's love can hurt sometime; it can also *bleed.*
I had so much to learn, you had so much to teach;
I can still hear your voice whispering,
"Boy, you better preach."

Although you are not *here*, I know you can never be gone,
but I do understand why the Father
called you home!

So go ahead my old sweet love; go
ahead and take your sleep.
Because I know I can do all things through Christ Jesus
that strengthens me.

For one day, heaven is where I want to be.
But until my time ceases, *Lord!*
I can't wait to see your blessing face.
Oh, holy Saint Chanie, "mother of grace."
Ashes to ashes and dust to dust,
"Pray for us!"

The Gospel Truth

O' Lord, hold back the clouds, and give me a rainbow sign.
Now it's my time, so God, let your sun shine.
Like the mouth of that fish, everything I spit is money.
Now watch and pray for me Pete, and don't sleep.
The truth flowing like milk and honey.

I can't subtract the word or add the word, but I can
divide it eight ways to Sunday. I'm coming like Jesus
came, just shining like a beacon, light so bright just
might blind you, deacon. So let me be God's witness
that his grace and mercy abide; like the sun, stars,
and moon, let me rise to testify. Let me rise.
Let me rise; let me rise to testify.

I'm going to lift up my voice and make a loud sound,
and I won't stop until Jericho's walls come down!
I need to be loud because the Holy Ghost set the tone.
Plus, my heart keeps the beat to the rhythm of this poem.
Lord, I prepare each day for this spiritual fight.

So let the words of my mouth be accepted in your sight.
Sometimes, the battle is lost although it might seem.
O' Lord, you are my strength and my redeemer.
Because my mama planted the seed way down low,
baptize it with water, and watch it grow.

She said, "Let's go to church and do work," that's where it begins.
So I took a pen and started writing away my sins.
I pray it brings me closer to heaven's door. So one day
I can say, "I wrote my name on heaven's row."
So let's go "back to church," just in time for devotion.

"Church is on fire!" Now, that's poetry in motion.
Jesus done paid the cost on the cross, so we have
no fee. It was his divine design for salvation,
"so give us free!" God so love the world that he shows
us in many ways. If shivery was dead, then he was
raised in three days.

I know the devil won't like this one,
but that one don't matter, so let God arise and
his enemies be scattered into the four winds, shattered
by the sun into obliteration. In the words of the
Holy One, "It is finish," and I'm done!

The Poet Praise

I will bless the Lord at all times; that's what my Bible says.
Because my God's grace continues to amaze; now, listen to a
    poet praise.
I don't need a sound check because God is my intro.
He said, "Open up your mouth, and speak, and let the Holy
    Ghost outflow."
I must do the will of my Father, and my Father's will I must do.
May his peace be upon you, be now unto you, bear witness
    to the truth.

For him indeed is the perfect love I found, but so heavy is
    the head
that wears the crown. Every day, I carry my cross; every day,
    my soul weep.
There can't be one lesson in a victory, but one thousand in defeat.
When you looking for Jesus, you looking for me.
He is in I, and I am in he; he is my Father; I am his son.
Me and the Holy Ghost and the Father are one.

And yes, he is the "Great Surgeon," with the great balm in
    Gideon.
He is the "Anointed One"; better run, devil; better run, run.
Jesus's name is the sweet sound that ring, ring. I can't blow a note,
but Lord, I can make my poetry sing, sing. I'm preaching with

fire and brimstone, and Lord, I'm smoking, the devil's screaming,
"Oh no! Now, who in hell left my gate open?

You see, I'm enticed by the Holy Ghost, with the power to
    hold and roll the sea back
like Moses. Many were called, but only one was chosen.
Now, pronounce the name Jesus, are you can pronounce it
    Ha'zoose.
But in his mighty name, I can pronounce you loose.
I want to give the Lord a poet praise, with my mind, body,
    and soul.
Excuse me, I want be a man of God if I didn't tip my hat to
    Sister Maya Angelou.

You see, I came to spread the good news, like Brother
Langston Hughes. Because Jesus done paid my way with zero
    balance,
that's why I can stand here with zero malice. I'm just trying to
give my God the must; you can call me "Paul Laurence Dunbar,"
with the Holy Ghost.

The Living Well

Psalm 40:3

O' Lord thou God, thou Creator of thee.
O' bless me now, O' Lord, for my soul thirst for thee.
So I come, O' Lord; I come to the well.
Just one drink of that well of living water and I'll believe,
And I'll thirst no more. For that well water flows so free.
So I come, O' Lord; I come to the well.
I come to the waters, the everlasting waters,
Where that well runs so deep.
I come to the waters, the everlasting waters,
Where my soul thirst for thee.
So I come, O' Lord I come to the well.
(Repeat chorus)

Oh' there's healing in this well, healing in this well,
Healing in this well for me.
Oh' there's love in this well, love in this well,
Love in this well that runs deep.
Oh' there's joy in this well, joy in this well,
Joy in this well for me.
Oh' there's peace in this well, peace in this well,
Peace in this well that runs deep.

Oh' there's grace in this well, grace in this well,
Grace in this well for me.
Oh' there's mercy in this well, mercy in this well,
Mercy in this well that runs deep.
There's life in this well, life in this well,
Life in this well for me.
Oh' Jesus is this well, Jesus is this well,
Jesus is this well that runs deep.
So I'll thirst no more for that water fills my soul,
Where water from that well flows free.

My Reflection

"When I look up in the sky, what do I see?" is a reflection of myself looking down at me.

"The sun, the moon, even the deep blue sea" is a reflection of the one that created me. "The stars in the heavens that shine so bright at night" is a reflection of myself that I see in sight.

"The four winds that blow in my face is felt," is just another reflection that I see in myself.

"The flowers and the trees that flow in the breeze so swiftly" is a reflection of myself that I see in me.

"The mountains and the streams, the birds that sing, and all those little bitty creepy crawling things" is a reflection of myself that I looked upon and seen.

My Testimony

I was born a Black child in the ghetto, is where my life began. I was introduced to hardship and poverty, iniquity, and sin. Everything was hand-me-down, and nothing was brand-new. First of all, it was secondhand. Everything was just used, everything down from my hat and my coat, my socks, and my shoes.

The life I had was hard and tough. That's all I can say. Mama said, "If you listen to me and just believe, the Lord will make a way." So I just wanna thank my mama for teaching me how to pray. I also like to thank the Lord for his mercy and grace.

You see, I can't even convey, so just let me lift my hands to worship and praise. Although nothing was easy and everything seemed so hard, Lord, you said, "The steps of a good man are ordered by God." Even though I had to cry sometimes, I knew if I just stayed on the grind, heaven will be mine.

Lord, I appreciate my path and the steps I took even though we hardly had any food to cook. But you kept on being gracious and providing for me even though my eyes were blurry and I couldn't see.

But, Lord, you still made it possible for me to dream. Now, I know and understood that all things work together for my good. Even though I wrote and started this page, *God, you are the author and finisher of my faith.* Lord, you protected me in the midst of my misery, and now, I'm forever thankful for my testimony.

Only God Knows

Somewhere up there, I heard the words "what's in the dark will soon come to the light." Things you never dreamt of will soon be in sight. Those behind closed doors will simply be exposed. Whether you're high or low, only God knows. You may be rich, or you may be poor, but the words I speak, you just can't ignore. Life is up, and sometimes, it's down.

There are peaks and valley that you can't get around. Things may flow wherever the wind blows. Where they go, only God knows. Angels are around us and surround us in droves. They are assigned to protect us and watch over our souls. Where they fly or float, only God knows. A fool will rush in where Angels won't even tread, just words to the wish where fearless feet have fled.

God created the heavens and then created earth and shaped us all from clay and dirt. He created humanity to give us all humility. That's why God is so worthy and so precious to me. I often wonder why, and what made him stoop down from high? And what is it about man that God keeps in mind? I really can't understand how it all goes, but what I can comprehend, only God knows.

Pennies from Heaven

Oh' how I wish upon a midnight star that pennies rain down from heaven near and far. Could it be the most pennies that I ever seen? Is this a reality, or is it a dream? I will take each penny a make wish. I will wish for kindness, peace, and happiness. I will use my second wish to eradicate hate. This world can use more love for heaven's sake.

But God's love can never be bought. That's just another shiny penny for your thought. I will use my third wish to feed the needy. There will be no such thing as hungry or greedy. I will heal the sick and give sight to the blind. I will give them clothes and shoes, and just let my light shine.

Pennies from heaven, oh' what a wonderful dish. Pennies from heaven, oh' how I wish. Pennies from heaven comes straight from the heart. It's love that is shared from the soul of God. Pennies from heaven represents "prosperity, along with faith, hope, grace, and charity."

Phone Prayer

Ring, ring, it's a phone call. I wonder who could it be? It's Mama and Sister Combs on the phone praying for me. She's asking the father just to bless her seed, my brother and sister, my nephew, and niece. Now, she pauses for the cause to pray for world peace. It's dawning, and I'm up early in the morning, stretching and yawning.

But it's me O Lord. I'm standing in the need of prayer. I need you to intercede, I'm in desperate need or care. I just wanna thank you Lord, for this intercessory prayer. If you want your city safe, better call the prayer line while it's not too late. Just call in now, and talk to your creator. Dial him up to reach the real operator.

The clock goes ticktock. It doesn't stop. There's no time to lose. The phone line is open if you need clothes and shoes. If you're in a mess and you feel stressed and alone, Jesus is on the main line. Just tell him what you want. Just open your mouth, and close your eyes. Just trust and believe that God specializes.

Body aches and heartbreaks and your bills are due. Why don't you call him on up and get your breakthrough? Old things shall pass away, and he'll make all things new. So leave your worries on the altar for he cares for you. Now, the clock on the wall says, "five-fifteen." It's time to eradicate the virus called COVID-19.

Lord, we pray right now in this very hour that you send us your Holy Ghost power. We pray that it doesn't prevail, and we send it back down to the depths of hell. Because it so evil and detrimental, that's why phone prayer is so essential.

It's six o'clock on the dot, and the phone line is hot. It's time to wash my face. I thought the praying was over. Now, they pick up the pace. Ring, ring, it's another call. I wonder what they'll say. It's Sister Kate on call wait, now the prayings on three-way."

Portrait of a Poet

Take a look at me, and tell me what you see. Does the complexity of me define who I'll be, or would the simplest thing you see be the best of me? God had no blemish, so he created me in his own image. I can recite you poetry and express my life through you. But can you hear the words I say and then see it through?

I wonder will the children I raise see better days than I? Will they be able to live, learn, or even fly? If I had a chance to do it all again, will I still be bold to reach out and touch the wind? I'm just a wordsmith that is equipped with grander penmanship, who's blessed with God's grace, who was given a gift to articulate prepositional phases.

Paper is my canvas, and a pencil is my brush. Words are my paint that you can feel and touch. You see, I was set apart from you just to impart this art that I do. It's just blessing to know what makes my creation flow. It comes from God, all creativity that comes from my heart. I can show you my life through the eyes that I see, but if I told you my life, I know you won't believe me. I've had storms and rain, heartaches, and pain.

But the Lord sustained me without blemish or blame. He allowed me to keep breathing and just keep on interceding. But Mama told me to don't be remiss and promised there'll be days without bliss. She told me to keep holding on to God's hand and keep trusting in his master plan.

She said, "Always pray without cease, and one day you'll be his masterpiece, just a beautiful portrait of a poet that's complete. I hope what I've shown you about me is everything you hoped to see and all that I'm known to be. The portrait I give is the poetry that I live and the poet that lives in me.

Preacher Man

Hell is a place you put liars and thieves. "You can do all things through Christ if you just believe." Strong words from a man who's standing on the corner with a Bible in his hand." The word around town is he's the Preacher Man. He preaches about the Holy Ghost, the Father, and the Son, screaming, "Whosoever will let him come."

He says, "God is good, and he can make you whole. Just give him a chance. He will save your soul while showing no fear by saying it bold." He's asking the Father to just give him a sign while laying hands on sick and healing the blind, screaming, "No more water but fire next time!"

People are looking and listening and trying to understand. The word around town is he's the Preacher Man. His words are being spoken on another level. He's telling the truth and shaming the devil. Mama and Daddy, if you spear that rod, you're gonna spoil that child.

Preacher says, "Sounds like the same song." But God bless the child who got his own, and God bless the parent that corrects the wrong. He preaches like a street corner Paul the Apostle full of the gospel, hanging on every word God says, proclaiming the just shall live by faith.

He says, "God is love. Let me count the ways," while holding up a poster that says, "Jesus saves!" He's a bona fide soul seeker and a hellfire-breathing preacher. People are coming from miles just to hear him speak. No money, no fame, only souls he seeks. Pounding his Bible like he was born to preach, he extends his hand toward heaven, and now he's pointing while speaking the truth with such great anointing.

The Holy Ghost flows through his veins, like an electrical infusion, like he was connected to the cross with a blood transfusion. Yea, you couldn't tell me that his power wasn't real. I felt the joy of the Lord as I was wiping my tears. People are looking and listening and trying to understand. The word around town is he's the Preacher Man.

Revelation

Run, sinner, run. The world is about to cease. Better run to the hills before destruction is released. If it's no Jesus, then it can be no peace. Everywhere you turn and face, it's earthquakes in diver places. I try to cover my ears to drown out the noise for all rumors and rumors of wars. Now, there's nothing I can do or say to get you ready for judgment day.

Now, it's just too late to even repent or pray. Just picture the stars in the sky fall like Jericho's wall did. Imagine and visualize while your whole body is paralyzed. Now, you're shakin' your knees. Your eyes are dilated, and now, you're gnashin' your teeth. The devil's ready to feast. It's the sign of times. Now, here comes the beast.

Triple six is real, no more coins or dollar bills. You're gonna need that seal if you wanna deal. Now, who can you trust? Only God can reveal. Sleepless nights are saturated in lust and sin. If sleep is the cousin to death, then that makes you kin. You can't tell the day from the night and summer from the winter bites.

Now, tell me who's the Antichrist? It's no more Bible vacation. It's the manifestation of revelation. In the phase of the last days, it will be unbearable sins that make you cringe. Men will love one another and women each other. It's hard to believe it will be the trend. There will be no more salvation. Now, it's just hell and damnation. What can we do? I hope God can save you.

It's just a pity. I'm just trying to get to the holy city. So I can see Trinity, Lord of Host." Translation: the Father, Son, and Holy Ghost. The first and the last, the beginning and the end, the Alpha and Omega, the Savior of my sins.

Now, the lamb is behold, who was found worthy to open the scroll. I see seven angels blowing seven trumpets loud. Now, I can see the Son of Man coming in the clouds. And we shall be caught up with him in a twinkle of an eye, and the dead in Christ will rise when that bright and morning star cracks the skies.

Now, you realize as you visualize and you're captivated by the truth. It's no place to run under the sun or the moon as you're trying to elude. It's just a general observation from where it begins to the end and from Genesis to Revelation.

Rise and Shine

I woke up this morning just at half past dawn. I couldn't wait to pray and thank God for the morning sun. With worship and praise, I rise and shine to wash my face. Thanking God for his mercy, thanking God for his grace, I rise and shine giving God the glory. I rise and shine to testify my story.

You see, I've been scandalized and criticized. But thank God I was baptized. I went down in muddy waters, but now, I rise. I've been used and abused and falsely accused. My life was filled with gloom and doom, but I rise and shine like the stars and the moon.

So what about me that you don't approve? That God had the audacity to bless me too. Plus, my success has equaled you. Did his generosity make you blue? While you keep looking at me with your piercing eyes, I'll still rise and shine like the sun in the skies. So fabricate your stories, and tell your vicious lies. But just like the blue sea, still, I rise.

I'll keep rising to the top. I'll keep rising like the wind, reaching the highest mountain rock. Yes, just like the wind, I'll rise, arms lifted toward heaven skies. Spread like a bird's wings, I fly. Yes, I'll rise. Hallelujah, I'll rise.

Sanctify Shack

Let's go down by the river, through the woods and in the back. There was an old tiny tin rooftop sanctify shack. It was something that if I told you, you wouldn't believe. They had drums and horns, washboards, and tambourines. Piano was in the corner playing different notes, and I just couldn't never forget those guitar strokes. So I said to myself, "O Lord, it's on."

Then Sister Combs started singing her song. That's when Brother Jones started blowing his trombone. Now, trust and believe it really took me back. It was Holy Ghost jubilee in this little sanctify shack. God has to anoint this joint because spiritual music was sinking in tune, and nothing sounded more smooth than that washboard and spoon.

The shack was hotter than a woodburning stove that was burning coal. I needed some water just to cool my soul. They did the sanctify dance all the way to cannon land, and folks were jumping up and down waving church fans. The floors started to crack, and there was nothing held back in this little sanctify shack.

I once was lost, but now, I'm a believer. I think I caught that sanctified fever. It was something that I couldn't avoid because everything that had breath was praising the Lord. I tell you this shack was really rocking because everybody was hopping. I knew they wasn't joking because that microphone started smoking when these words were spoken, y'all the doors to church are open!

Sanctuary

The atmosphere is set, and the mode is right. The spirit of the Lord is about to move tonight. The saints are assembled, and we are ready for this phase. God, we need your mercy and your grace to amaze. So we enter into the sanctuary with worship and praise.

So let me just simply say that the presence of the Lord is truly in this place. I can see the spirit of the Lord on each and every face. Now God, we're ready and waiting on you. We're elating and anticipating on what you're gonna do. Miracles are in the air, and blessing is falling like rain. I can feel the joy of the Lord as the worship choir sang.

God we are here, and we wanna do your will. Just speak to us Lord, and the sick will be healed. Our hands are raised high, and we are ready to receive. Nothing is impossible if you only believe. Everybody is soul searching, and spiritual gifts are working. It's all necessary, and nothing is ordinary, and you'll never be the same in this holy sanctuary.

Six Black Crows

Six black crows were sitting in a tree, looking down at a car-cass that they just might eat. The first crow said, "Oh, what a treat, let's pick the bones and carve the meat." The first black crow said, "What do you see?"

The second crow said, "I see a lost soul just looking up at me, with no hope, no joy, no love, and no peace. My oh my, what a wonderful feast." The second black crow said, "What do you see?"

The third crow said, "I see storms and rain, heartaches and pain, just a lost soul who's trying to sustain." The third black crow said, "What do you see?"

The fourth crow said, "I see grace and mercy and what I hope can be, because God is so mindful of even black birds in a tree." The fourth black crow said, "What do you see?"

The fifth crow said, "I see faith, hope, and charity. God is always gracious when his creatures are in need." The fifth black crow said, "What do you see?"

The sixth crow said, "I see sunny days and pretty blue skies, no more distrust and no more lies, just a delightful soul looking up at me, with nothing but love, joy, and prosperity, because God is so faithful to even a black bird like me."

Spiritual Mind

Let me remind you spiritually that it's good to imagine and wonder, but wonder and imagine what can you do with a good spiritual mind?" Could you dream the impossible dream? Would you talk about words that the ears have never heard or see things that the eyes have never seen? Will you heal the sick and give sight to the blind? Will you walk on water or turn water into wine?

So tell me what would you do with your spiritual mind? Could you sing like an angel and set the captive free? Would you command the four winds or calm the seven seas? Will you speak to a disease and make demons flee? Could you play an instrument with a spiritual finesse while guided by the Holy Spirit like you were possessed?

Will somebody get delivered from something you said while you were spreading the gospel like it was a plague? Would you give hope and faith to a nonbeliever while you're rebuking the deceiver and casting out evil? Could you forsake yourself to do God's will, speak to the heavens, and make time stand still? Would you pray in tongues, interpret wonders and signs?

So tell me what will you do with your spiritual mind? In the beginning, the Word was told, "Love the Lord your God with your mind, body, and soul." Search the scriptures, and you will find "be ye transformed by renewing of your mind." The devil likes to play on his ground, so guard your mind, and keep it sound.

If you got faith of a mustard seed, this is what you can do. Speak to a mountain, and the mountain will move. You can speak to a storm, and the storm will cease. I just can't even explain my thesis because this is spiritual telekinesis. So let your mind be in you, which was also in Christ Jesus.

Tent Revival

Hurry up, saints, and go get your Bibles." The end-time has come, and it's about survival. Lord, bring us old-time tent revival. O Lord, we need a fresh anointing of your power. We need a Holy Ghost tent revival. So kick that sawdust off your shoes. Now, praise him in the dance with harps and flutes, from the rising of the morning to breaking of the dawn. Praise be the Lord, with symbols and drums.

I will worship the Lord all my days. Now, lift your voices with songs of praise. Light your oil, and turn up your lamps. Now, this is what you call a tent revival camp. Saints and sinners are being slanged, drenched by the Holy Ghost rain. So fill up our cups Lord, and let them overflow until our souls are full and we thirst no more.

Now, let the redeemed of the Lord say it's so. When you touched me O' Lord, I knew I wasn't the same. I knew without a shadow of doubt that I've been changed. So let that rock of ages care for me as I hide myself deep in thee. One thing is for sure, and I know it for certain. You can put your troubles on the altar and forget about your burdens. I know a place where the blood will never lose its power. It's way down here at the old tent revival!"

The Pastor's Wife

There she goes, all deck in white sitting on the front row for show. She got her big hat that match the dress she wears that looks whiter than snow. Now, ain't she a mess? She gives you her Sunday best. But she is the worst when she curses on Thursday. Oh' she may be the prettiest thing you ever seen, but she can also be mean.

Some folks call her the pastor's wife, and other folks the church queen. Sometimes, she can be so quite without even saying a word. But you can trust and believe, and please take heed, that she also knows how to be heard. With the queen by his side, what can the pastor do? His first lady maybe, she stares at Sister Katy while giving her the unspoken rule.

She's always on guard for her man of God and any homestead intruder. Some preacher's wife was called, but this one he chose. Was she heaven sent? Only God knows. She's more concerned with her shoes and clothes, rather than saving lost souls. She tries to put a smile on her face, while she stands in the pastor's space trying to show grace.

But grace is a gift that comes from above. You'll the pastor's wife, but you don't show any love. The pastor has a tough task, trying to do the Master's will. But this pastor's wife will not suffice because she doesn't know how to forgive.

Wedding Anniversary

It seems like it was yesterday when you were my bride to be. Oh, what a blessed day that was, when you chose to marry me.

The splendor of your beauty was so truly hard to believe. My reaction to your attraction was so hard for me to perceive. It must've been a God above to trust me with your love. My love that I couldn't deny. I remember the day that I saw your face as you were gracious walking bye. So I pursued you as I alluded you as we looked in each other's eyes.

I condense you as I convinced you that I was your potential king. I was conveying you as I was swaying you that you were my initial queen. So I reminisce what I miss as I memorized the seen. So we connected, and now we were vested as I invited you into my life.

I was so bold to you when I told you then that you were going to be my wife. I was so intrigued as I sowed my seed and prayed you'll be the one. Someone I can build a house with and be a spouse with that will give me daughters and sons. Although I know our love had to grow, we started out as friends. I knew you will always be there for me, right down to the very end.

I will walk a mile to see you smile and to glance at your pretty face. No one can ever duplicate your style or your grace. There is no place that I wouldn't follow you under the heavens and the stars. I will always profess my love for you before the angels and God.

Our love we share doesn't even compare to any other loves before. The love we feel is so real. It will last one hundred years or more. I'm so sincere, thank you my dear, for every year that you'll given me. Now we are celebrating our wedding day and all that life can be. It's a very special occasion for it's our anniversary."

When Doves Cry

They say if you open up a bird cage and let doves fly, they will come back home after sailing the skies. They will fly through storms and rain, smoke, or even fire. But did you ever wonder why a dove cries? God sees the world through the eyes of a dove, often seeing good and bad, hate and even love.

The dove has no voice, but yet it can speak, often flying away to rest and always seeking peace. The wings of a dove are fragile but yet so strong, surviving forceful winds to carry the dove home. The dove has God's eyes and can see all things, whether near or far, "seen or unseen."

Noah used a dove to find dry land "after God cleanse the world with rain" and destroyed the kind of man. The dove flew and flew, but it found no rest. It just kept flying high and doing it's very best. After flying for days and weeks, God's eyes return with just a single olive leaf. Oh, what a sight it must've been as the dove flew by.

Can you see that dove in morning as he sadly arrived. But God's eyes are so merciful, and he delivered the promised land. He sent his only Son as a reconcile to man. When John baptized Hosanna, the heavens open wide. God's love came as a dove and descended down and cried."

Wicked Ways

Lord, cast me out to darkness for I am hated, until all my sins are obliterated. You said you'll destroy a wicked man's deed, but it's me oh' Lord, standing here in need. Nevertheless, I know you're just even though I often betrayed your trust. It's true. I've been remiss, but toss me into the sea of forgiveness.

Even though I chose evil over righteousness, Lord, I tried to forget the wrong that I've done because I was created in your image," and I'm still your son. Now, I know the ways of the wicked prosperous none. I was so elated to be persuaded by that wicked one.

Instead of eating the bread of life, I ate the bread of wickedness and strife. I was full of jealousy and greed, so I planted bad seeds. It grew strange fruits from the root of my wickedness tree. Lord, I don't confess to nothing that you didn't see, but turn not your face away from me.

I know you're still God, so create in me a new heart. I seek salvation, but you know I deserve hell and damnation. Lord, my iniquity, I have done wickedly. So sincerely, I repent to you all my wicked deeds, for you are God who numbers my days, and now, I can see the error of my wicked ways.

Barbershop

I went to the barbershop one day. I was in desperate need
of a haircut and a shave. I stood on the wall. Then I waited
until my number was called. So I boldly walked over and sat
in barber's chair, with my mangled and tangled intertwined
hair. My barber was tall and dressed all in white, but on his
face, there was a shining ray of light.

He greeted me with kindness by saying, "How do you
do? Is there anything in particular, sir, that I can do for you?"

I responded politely, "I'm really not sure, maybe a style
that folks can't ignore. Give me something that they haven't
seen if you know what I mean. Just cut it low on the sides
and medium in the back. Give me a high-top fade, but leave
it flat." Everyone that heard me talking smack knew that this
barbershop was packed.

He replied, "All right, sir, just sit back and relax." My
neck was taped to his barber's cape. Then he combed my hair
back. He said, "I'm really glad that you are here," while he
was leaning in closely and whispering in my ear. "It seems
you know what you want, and that's a fact, but there's something, my good man, that you just might lack. I think you are
kind and perceive to be nice. But do you have God in your
heart, and do you know Jesus Christ?"

I was really surprised of the question he gave, but I
needed to reply if I wanted to be saved. He said, "If you follow my instructions and take my advice, I will give you the

secrets to eternal life. If you think this just a little too much, trust me. I can provide you much more than a fancy haircut.

So I asked my barber, "How can this be?"

He said, "Close your eyes, sir, and repeat after me: 'Lord, right now in this barbershop, forgive me for my sins, and come into my heart. Lord, I confess that I'm a mess and my sins are great. But Lord, I know you died on a cross so I can be saved. God, I'm asking right now for your mercy and grace. Lord, I seek heaven and salvation even though I know I deserve hell and damnation.

'Lord, please forgive me for the wrong that I've done. I know I'm a sinner, but I'm still your son. Jesus, I know you made the ultimate sacrifice, for you are the way, the truth, and the life. God, your Holy Spirit I want to receive. You said that nothing is impossible if I only believed. Lord, I know you make all things new. I know there is no other way to your Father except by you.

'So Jesus, I accept you right now as my Lord and Savior. Thank you for your precious gift, and thanks for your favor.'"

When I open my eyes, I felt free from sin, so I softly spoke. Then I said, "Amen." I then asked my barber, "What do I owe?

He said, "Sir, it won't be any charge today you know."

I asked him, "Why?"

He then replied, "Because Jesus already paid the price a long time ago."

Baptism

I went down by the riverside, way down by the muddy stream. It seems like it was yesterday, oh, what a wonderful scene. Everybody was lined up in the water, all dressed up in white. Lord, I wish y'all could've been there, oh, what a glorious sight.

The preacher was standing in the deep, baptizing God's saints. The choir was singing, "Take me to the water," while they stood on the riverbank. "Repent, and be baptized!" That's what I heard him say. Now, if you do, I got proof that you can all be saved because it's only one Lord and one God, and there's only one faith.

So I step down in the cold water just as timid as I could be. He said, "Now, be baptized in the precious name of Jesus!" When I came up from the muddy river, my soul felt clean. I saw a beaming light, then I knew I was redeemed. Now, I'm on my way to heaven because my soul was set free. Lord, thank you for your grace and mercy and for baptizing me."

Beyond the Gates

Lord, lay me down to sleep. I pray to you my soul you'll keep, and if I die before I wake, give me safe passage beyond the gates. Sometimes I wonder what's my fate and what mysteries await me beyond the gates. When the breath I breathe is no more to take, I will gladly give for heaven's sake.

With visions of my mother standing at the gate and all my passed loved ones in wait. Sometimes, I ask God for a sign and wish the gates just open wide. But my hourglass is full inside, and only God holds the sands of time. But nevertheless, I digress because he always knows what's best. He's the one that numbers my days and nights, who turns my darkness into light.

So I will run until the race is done, until I'm victorious and I have won. Yet I will go on trying to be strong, still fixated on the unknown. But am I wrong to imagine kneeling at the throne and bowing down at the King's feet who sacrificed for me?

So let me lift my hands and reach far beyond the stars where there's no more pain and grief, where there's no more deceit and hate. It's way up there in the stratosphere beyond the gates. I can't hardly believe that's where I'll spend my eternity, and time won't even mind because forever is my destiny."

Black Angel

When I'm walking along and no one is walking beside me, I feel a strange loving presence that I get behind me. I look to my left. Then I look to my right. There is a dark shadow that I can see in sight.

Now, I know a shadow can often be seen. But this shadow of mine has a pair of wings. My shadow guides my steps wherever I need to go, and it always tells me whatever I need to know. I can't believe how my shadow intercedes and always watching over me as I slumber and sleep. It protects me from the grim reaper as he sneaks and creeps.

Now, most shadows often appear at night, but this shadow of mine of often appears in the light. Sometimes, it takes flight and most times disappears. But whenever I'm in fear, my shadow reappears. And wherever I'm in need, it will be there indeed.

My shadow covers me. It's my guiding light. Whenever it's with me, my future looks bright. My shadow protects me from clear and present danger. Wherever I'll be, I'll take it with me. It's my beautiful black guardian angel.

Black Jesus

What color was Jesus? Does anyone know? Was he from Bethlehem or a Birmingham ghetto? His skin was like bronze. It's what we were told. What color was Jesus? Was he a negro? His hair was like wool for what they can see. Was it straight, long, curly, or was it nappy like me? His eyes were like fire. It's what we were told.

He wasn't even desired. Was he a negro? What color was Jesus? Does anyone know? Was he from Bethlehem or a Birmingham ghetto? What color was Jesus? Was he a negro? Could he really heal the sick and give sight to the blind? Did he walk on water? Would he turn water into wine?

What color was Jesus? Does anyone know? Was he from Bethlehem or a Birmingham ghetto? What color was Jesus? Does anyone know? What color was Jesus? Was a he negro? Did he really calm the storm? Could he really cease the rain? Does he really give you peace? Would he really cease your pain?

What color was Jesus? Does anyone know? Was he from Bethlehem or a Birmingham ghetto? What color was Jesus? Does anyone know? What color was Jesus? Was he a negro? Could he really raise the dead? Did he feed five thousand with five loaves of bread? Would he save the lost? Was he tried and convicted just to die on the cross?

What color was Jesus? Does anyone know? Was he black, white, red, or was he yellow? What color was Jesus?

Does anyone know? What color was Jesus? Was he a negro? Just look at me, and tell me what you see. Could my blessed Savior be black like me? Just look at me, and look at me hard. Can a negro actually be the Son of God?…

Blind Faith

Now, faith is the substance of things hoped for, the evidence of things not seen. Sometimes, that can be hard. With men, that is impossible but not so with God. If you can believe, all things are possible to him, who can open his hands and receive. Then all things are possible to him, who can close his eyes and believe.

What can be more precious to a man than what his eyes can see? But blessed is the man that hears to word and have faith enough to believe. Your faith doesn't have to be big or obese. There is really not a need. Your faith can be tiny or small, something just like seed. Jesus did not heal the blind man because he could not see; it was because he could not see, but yet he still believed."

Savior of My Soul

Once there was a man that fell off a ship into the ocean and was floating in the sea. But a man came along that was driving a speedboat that was just passing by.

He saw him floating in the water, so the man said, "Give me your hand, and I will help pull you out of the water."

But the man refused and said, "No, that's okay. I'm just waiting on God to save me."

So the man in the boat just passed him on by. So the man just kept floating in the water. Some hours went by, and still, the man was waiting. So a man in a helicopter was flying by and saw the man floating in the sea and threw him down a rope ladder.

So the man flying the helicopter said, "Climb the rope ladder, and I will pull you out of the water."

But the man again refused and said, "No, that's okay. I'm just waiting on God to save me."

So the man in the helicopter just flew on by him. So the man got tired of floating in the water. Finally, he gave up, and so the man drowned.

Then he went to heaven. Finally, the man saw God. So the man said, "Lord, I was waiting on you to come and save me before I died, but you never came."

So God replied, "Oh, but I did, my son. I sent you a boat and a helicopter."

Although this story is very much fictional, the moral to it means, God often comes in many shapes and forms. He is the master of disguises. As a believer, you must be able to recognize him in all his grander glory."

Church Boy

When I was a little boy, my mama took me to church. She said, "If you want to go to heaven, you first got to work."

I said, "Mama, I'm just a boy. What can I do?"

She said, "You can sweep up the floor son, then wipe down the pews. When you get through and all finished with that, you can put on your coat and hat. Walk up the street boy, and then pass out tracks.

"When you complete that assignment, this is what you must do. Go tell the people on the corner about Sunday school. You must be bold son, and you can't be weak. Just open up your mouth, and then God will speak. Now be good, and learn your Easter speech. So don't you worry son God is always near, because his perfect love cast out all fear.

"But if you only fear God, one day you'll be wise. Now a wise man boy is what evil despise. I know you're just a boy, but you're growing up fast. Remember, 'what you do for Christ would only last.' Now, please don't forget to cut the church's grass.

"So let God use you for heaven's sake. You can hang up the choir robes or collect the money plates. To do God's will, boy you got to have zeal, and don't forget that he has the power to heal and give sight to the blind, and if you seek the truth, then the truth you will find. God wants to use you boy in this very hour. He wants to give you passion, purpose, and power.

"If you can believe it, you can achieve it. Just lift your hands, and you can receive it. When you walk with Christ, you must walk a tightrope. And don't ever forget about faith, charity, and hope. God will give you everything you will need to do his will. So take this Bible. This is your sword and shield. Your mouth is a weapon, and it can be powerful my son, because the power of life and death is in the power of your tongue.

"And never forget boy, you reap what you sow, and whatever you reap, God will anoint it to grow. To be a good soldier, you got to be able to fight. So be strong in the Lord and the power of his might. So never let the devil steal your joy, and one day, you will make a wonderful church boy."

Christmas Card

I got a Christmas card in the mailbox today. I hurry up to open it just to see what it say. It simply said, "Warm wishes to you in this festive holiday season, and never forget that Jesus is always the reason." It indeed expressed to me that all my hopes and dreams come true and may all things that are old now and forever become new.

Such a wonderful card brought good tidings and joy. The joy that brings love to the world for every little girl and boy. On this Christmas day, I was so happy to convey about this very special card. Oh, I wish you could've heard the most beautiful words, that must've come straight from the mouth of God.

Christmas is a special day that comes once a year. We all celebrate the birth of our Lord that is so precious and dear. Such a wonderful card, I knew it came straight from above, but the greatest gift God has given us is his perfect gift of love. Christmas represents love, peace, joy, and cheer. It is the most beautiful and wonderful time of the year.

People are sharing presents and roasting chestnuts in a barrel. While the children are outside dressed in their hats and coats singing old Christmas carols, the men are shoveling ice and snow in escapade from the driveway to the wall. While some are having fun playing, just throwing white snowballs, the women are in the house hanging red bows and mistletoes, while some are standing by the fireplace just singing, "Let it snow. Let it snow."

Oh, I just can't believe that Christmas is finally here. It's the most beautiful and wonderful time of the year. Families are gathered, getting ready for Christmas dinner. Oh, what a wonderful finale for a long-awaited winter. So I thank them for my card, and I politely addressed the sender. Yes, the birth of our Lord is so precious and dear. So Merry Christmas to you all and, to you all, a (happy New Year).

Church on Fire!

"Church on fire!" That's what I heard somebody shout, but there's something really strange. Nobody's trying to put it out. Let it burn! Let it burn!" That's what I heard somebody scream. The temperature's so high even I can feel the steam. I ran up the street and open up the church door, oops! There it is. Somebody done hit the floor as if somebody was told, "Hey, just stop, drop, and roll."

I ran down the aisle. I started getting a funny feeling. The room is full of smoke, and flames are coming from the ceiling." A man walked up to me, whom I never seen before, and started talking about an invisible man or some kind of Holy Ghost.

A lady in the corner started singing a church song, talking about, "It's just like fire shut up in my bones!" So I ran over to her just to see what I can do. She said, "Son, you're not here to help me, but you are here for me to help you."

She started speaking to me in an unfamiliar tongue. Now she's taking about the Holy Ghost, the Father, and the Son. Now all of a sudden, I started to run. It was like somebody had pulled a fire alarm because I ran out the church, and then I ran back in. As the choir started singing, "He will wash your sins." Somebody grabbed me by the arm and put me in a seat, but I can't sit down because there's heat in my feet.

It started in the feet and went all the way up my legs. The heat kept going. Now, the heat is in my head. The more the choir sung. The more the fire got fed. Now, I'm down on my knees just crying to be saved. Spitting flames out my mouth with a Holy Ghost praise, I can't help myself. I'm in a Holy Ghost daze.

Then I got up because I was burned up, and I was consumed by this blaze. As I was thanking God Eternal for this gospel inferno, a preacher came up to me and asked me again, "Do the fire inside warm the cold that was in? Never mind that question. I see your face for it glows and shines with God's mercy and grace.

"Now my son you truly have something to tell, because God's fire inside of you burns hotter than the devil's fire inside of hell. Yes, the church is on fire, but please don't be overly concerned. You can tell me again and again, and I will tell you…let it burn! Let it burn!"

Crown of Thorns

They scold and scowl me and call me king. It's all hell for you sire, it's what they scream. I often seek peace, but instead, they throw sticks and stones at the throne of the king's feet. So there's no peace in the valley where I'll sleep. It's none to be found So heavy is the head that wears the crown, so henceforth, shall I suffer more? So shall I never reign without pain? And there can be no sunshine without rain.

I can't even count the cost that I lost, but still, I will bear my cross because I have a deep burning desire to go higher, but what's a sacrifice without fire? I have no regrets. The higher I go, the deeper it gets. So I emerged from the flames saved and unscathed because fortunes will forever favor the brave.

I will accept all malice just to walk on the streets of gold and to see my palace. I won't cease until I'm done, then will I see my father, which is in heaven, and then will my kingdom come. I know I've been worn, but strip and stripe me until I'm scorn until my body bleeds and I'm torn, but fatefully, I will wear my crown of thorns.

Crucifixion

On that dark and dreary, dreadful day, I never could've imagined my Lord would've suffered that way. Oh' Mary his mother started to weep, as the good shepherd was being led to slaughter and sacrificed like a sheep. Ancient prophecy was revealed as the crucifixion of our Lord was now being fulfilled.

So they beat him at will as he stumbled and staggered up Golgotha's hill. But not all was lost because like Simon, we all must bear his cross. So he was wounded for our transgressions. Oh yes, that was the cost. He was brushed for our iniquities, and still, the chastisement of peace was upon him, and by his stripes, we are healed.

They nailed his feet and hands. He was crucified with two rebels, this holy righteous Man. Even though it was painful and everyone was sad, he knew everything was going according to plan. The elders taunted him and flaunted him out loud. "If he's truly the Christ," they said, "let God rescue him now."

They hung his cross up high as darkness covered the sky, and it must've seemed like hours. He was slowly fading away as the day went astray. He was rapidly losing his power. His body was badly beaten and torn, and a cloak around his head was a keen crown of thorns. It was a mean grisly scene. Some say that day was worse than most.

That was when he bowed his head and took his last breath, then he gave up his Ghost. Now, Caiaphas thought it was all over when Pilate crucified Jehovah. But my Savior had everything to gain and nothing to lose. His final charge was written, this is Jesus, King of the Jews.

Daddy's Girl

Lord, I just can't believe what you have given to me. She is so pretty with little curls. Oh, would it be? Oh, could it be that she is Daddy's baby girl? Lord, I like to thank you indeed for blessing me and delivering such a precious gift. But time will come and go so swift that she will soon let go of my hand.

Oh' Lord, I pray to you that she surely receives a spiritual godly man. But until that time comes, it will be so fun to watch my baby girl grow. But in the meantime, she's all mine to love, cherish, and hold. I will protect her and comfort her and rock her little soul.

When I first saw her lying there, oh, how much she must've wept. I can't believe how far she's come to take her little steps. Oh, she's the most precious thing I've ever seen, and I'm sure you will agree. Imagine if you went to heaven and saw a baby with wings. She's the sun, the stars, and the moon and the center of my world. She will be forever to me, whenever I see, Daddy's baby girl.

Dry Bones

I rose from burning ashes. I came up from the deep. Death couldn't conquer me. I was immune to sleep. My life was so perplexed. I didn't know what was next. Everything was so dark and dreary, and it was so complexed. It's just my reflection of my affliction. That's just how I feel. I was in the valley of dry bones, and I couldn't get healed.

But I heard a voice from heaven that was so loud and clear that asked me a question, "Can these bones live?" So I made up mind that I wasn't going to die. Just like the prophet Ezekiel, I began to prophesy.

So come breath from the four winds, breathe down from the sky. Breathe life into these dry bones where these dry bones lie. My bones started to rattle, and my legs began to shake. My body was gyrating like it was an earthquake. I was tried by fire, and I was molded like gold. See what the Lord has done?

Now, look upon and behold. You see, I got all new features because if any man be in Christ, he is a new creature. So death, where is your sting, and where is your mean bite?" Because I refused to go softly into the dead of night. Now, there's no more moans and groans. Now I only sing spiritual songs, in the valley of the dry bones.

Freedom

Freedom…my county, 'tis of thee, sweet land of liberty, was the decoration that was declared to me. But did you know that Jesus was the reason that made us free? Long, long before four scores and seven years ago, Jesus died on the cross. Many, many years are more. Before Abraham Lincoln declared us free, Jesus said, "Whoever the Son set free, is free indeed."

So to me, this is why we sing. This is why Liberty Bell rings. Our Lord and Savior died, is the reason why freedom cried. So from every mountain side, let freedom ring because freely, he gave us all things, and freely, the water of life springs. Salvation is what it brings, and this is what it means…freedom.

Now, the Lord is a spirit, and where the spirit of the Lord is, there is freedom for freely, he gave his love to me, and for freedom, Christ has set us free. For you were called to freedom, my brothers, so don't get caught up in your mess, with opportunities of the flesh.

Only keeping your eyes on thee, and you will know the truth, and the truth will set you free. Because God shared his love, freedom is what freedom does because we can walk down the street, with no chains on our hands and no chains on our feet.

I only just can look up toward heaven and weep. So long may our land be bright with freedom's holy light. Protect us from all things, great God our King. Our Lord, so strong and true, I just want to thank you…for freedom.

Fishers of Men

Go cast out my nets across the sea. I'm fishing for fish that can feed my sheep. Take your boats out where the waters are deep. Search the hills and mountains below the sea. And when you draw your fishes, then go draw some more. Spread your dragnets across the shore.

I know you fishermen like to fish at night, but a good fisherman can fish in the light. The waters are clear, and your catch is near. There's always fresh fish along the pier from the Sea of Galilee to the shores of Judea. Just open your eyes and believe. Now watch me work a miracle in the mist of the sea.

If you receive my divine plan, then you can catch fish on dry land. Always be relentless in your search, and on this rock, I'll build my church. Just trust in me to the upmost. Stop doubting and believe, and just step out the boat. "For the world is the sea; and you fishermen are disciples of me.

The fish that you hold in your hands represents the souls of man. The gospel that is told are your nets for the fold. And eternal life is the goal to get to the distant shores."

Flawless Flowers

Lord, thank you for your flowers for they are your flowers to give. I appreciate the flowers that you gave to us, while we all may live. The flowers that you gave to us look so precious and dear. The glory of the flowers you gave is the splendor of your rain. It was a gift of love that you brought to us to cover the heartaches and pain.

Your flowers have many names and faces. That makes them so unique to know. They are white tulips, blue begonias, and they are pretty little red roses. Your flowers can grow from the sunlight or can glow from the moon of night. But the assorted flowers we see are so adorable indeed. That makes them a glorious sight.

Thank you for your flowers Lord, that you gave us to behold. The beautiful flowers that you gave us, we often use to console. The fragrance of your flowers is truly something to tell. Lord, thank you for their delightful signs and for their wonderful smell."

Grace

Amazing grace, oh' how sweet that sounds. It was amazing grace that this wretched man found. Grace is a gift that comes from God, but receiving grace sometimes can be hard because grace is something that comes straight from the word. Grace is giving when we really don't deserve it. God gives us grace by his perfect will, but to give us grace, he first had to forgive.

That's why forgiveness for each other should be our mission. It's why God's grace to me is so sufficient. Because we were beautifully and wonderfully made, it's why God's grace is just so amazing. If God's love is blind, then so is his grace. So we shall seek God's grace, like we seek his face.

Oh' Lord, thy word is a lamp unto my feet. That's why your grace to me is just so sweet. God, when your light unto my path is not so clear, Lord, I won't be afraid, and I won't fear. Even in my darkest hour, I know you are near. When I chose a different path and I went my own way, thank you for your protection Lord, and covering me with your grace.

Even on the highest mountain or the lowest parts of the sea, I want to thank you Lord for protecting me with your grace and mercy. I once was lost, but thank God for finding me. I once was blind, but now, I can see. I went through many dangers, toils, and snares. But Father, I know that you were always there.

I know it was grace that brought me safe thus far. I just looked toward heaven, and I followed the stars. Lord, I thank you for the good that you promised me in that hour when I first believed. When your word for me I didn't receive and your love I often denied, Lord, you just kept on blessing me, and your grace just kept abiding."

Granny's Garden

In her secret little closet, very quiet and discreet, down on her bending knees, my granny prayed for me. My ear was pressed to the door, very soft as kept. I listened to my granny's prayer as she prayed when she wept. Lord, I'm kneeling down here so humble and meek. Lord, rain down on me, and bless my seed.

Shower down on me from my head to my toe. Saturate me with your love, and let my seed grow. When you finish with your rain, give me a rainbow sign. Now smile on me Lord, and let your sunshine. Create me flowers straight from my soul, until my pretty little flowers turn into beautiful big roses.

Lord, I know it won't be easy, and sometimes it may be hard. But fertilize my roses, and create me a rose garden. Shield them from the winds, and protect them from the storm. Cover them with thorns to keep them from harm.

I know bad weather will come, and dark days will loom. But bless my rose petals, and let them bloom. For they are my sons and they are my daughters, watch over them Lord, for you are the Potter. Guide them from right and wrong, and teach them what to say. Lord, I know they'll be willing in your blessed name I pray."

Hallelujah Highway

I was driving down a highway many years ago. I drove past a road sign that read, "Hallelujah 54." As I drove down the highway, I wondered where would it lead. I said to myself, "Well, I'll just see." I followed the road for miles, just to see where will it go. But I kept passing the sign that said, "Hallelujah 54."

So I just stayed on the highway because I wanted to see. I drove a few more miles just to see where it would lead. As I traveled down the highway, I passed a sign that read, "Salvation for Everyone, 100 Miles Ahead." I just kept on driving. I knew I was close to the end, but soon, I pass a road sign that said, "Detour to Sin." But I knew I couldn't go that way because I knew I'll be late.

The detour sign read, "Heavy Destruction and Hate." To get to my destination, I had to go straight. The speed limit was sixty-five, so I drove at a slow pace. I was studying as I rode because it wasn't a fast race. Although the roads got rough and the lanes got strange, the weather got tough, so many thunderstorms and rain.

But still, I traveled on because my path was set." I passed a yellow sign that said, "Slippery When Wet." It wasn't the kind of information that I wanted to know, but still, I traveled north on Hallelujah 54. As I drove on, I ran into a tough terrain. I passed a railroad crossing, and I saw the devil's train. I just kept on driving, and I followed all the arrows.

The road was no longer wide. It was winding and narrow. I knew I was very close, I didn't have many miles to go. I just kept traveling the road on Hallelujah 54. I drove so long and far, sometimes I thought I was lost, but finally I saw a sign that read, "One Bridge to Cross." So I drove over the bridge, just so happy as I can be. Finally, my journey was complete. Now, there's salvation for you and me.

Hell's Kitchen

The devil's in the kitchen cooking up something mean. He's slicing and dicing and chopping up some dreams. He's got a pot full of jealousy, chaos, and deceit, throw in a cup of hate, now that's his favorite recipe. Lies and envy can be some tough meat to chew, but it's the perfect combination for some bad devil's stew.

Now when it comes to confusion, he's the ultimate master. He knows this sour recipe is made for disaster. Distrust plus lust, it can ruin a man's soul, and revenge is a dish that the devil serves cold. With just the right mix, the devil can seal your doom. Then he'll step back and relax and then lick his spoon.

One cup of agony, two teaspoons of fake, put it all in, and just let it blind. Then he'll turn up the heat and bake." He likes looking at you all blue, cold, despaired, and sick. Now, he's cooking with grease in hot fire. Then he'll smile at you and spit.

All you preachers lying, deceiving, and cheating God's sheep, hell's kitchen is where you're gonna eat. While you're living so shady, slick, and sly, you'll get your slice of some misery pie. Now, fear is a flavor that you can't leave out. It always shows up in hell's kitchen with doubt.

Fear is a flavor that you got to recognize. It always appears in devil's food in disguise. The devil knows fear, and he can taste it well because fear is a factor that the devil can smell. But here is something that I need to mention, "Jesus went to hell and closed down the kitchen."

With a little bit of cinnamon and a whole lot of spice, he told the devil that he was the Bread of Life." And if anybody was hungry and wanted to eat, Jesus told them, "Follow me." If you are rich with good wealth or poor with bad health, the devil knows who's the master chef."

Holloway's Grocery Store

Let me take you to a place that you've never been before, deep down in the south to Holloway grocery store." Just close your eyes, and picture this view." It's 1954, at 5532 Norway Avenue." Now, people in this store were so gentle and kind. You really didn't mind spending a dollar or a dime. They were the kindest folks if you've ever wanted to meet 'em. You'll probably tip your hat if you had a chance to greet 'em.

They said, "Yes, ma'am," and "No, sir," and they spoke with country slurs. They used fine grammar with prepositional words. It was the pure epitome on how can you serve. Let's just say that it was a one-stop shop. People came from miles around. Lord, they shopped till they dropped.

Black folks and White folks are shopping in peace. It was something like heaven, where color was obsolete. They had cookies, cakes, candy, and pies, every sweet treat and wonderful surprise. They had hamburgers, pork chops, fish and ham hocks, chicken and neck bones, and tails from an ox. They had flour and sugar. There were milk and bread. They had cabbage and corn. There were potatoes and eggs.

Fish and grits were like country caviar, and can you give me those pig feet in jar? They had black-eyed peas and collard greens. Lord, it was the best mini market you've ever seen. They had every fruit that you wanted and dreamed; apples, oranges, bananas, and nectarines. Now, the honeydew is a very sweet melon, but the watermelon was the top selling.

It was something that you couldn't believe. Deep down south was our own little Garden of Eden." Cars and trucks are going zoom, trying to catch the latest boom, going and coming fast, trying to get twenty-nine cents gas.

Even though the days were slow, time soon passes. Ladies, they sold hot combs if your head was nappy and strong. Men, they sold hair grease if you wanted to slick your dome. This store was well-known, and yes, it was Black owned.

This little paradigm was ahead of its times. I thought it might be something to know since it was 1954 and color folks just didn't own "maw and paw" grocery stores. I only said that to say God can use whom he may to spread his love and grace.

As you came in and shopped around awhile, up and down the aisles, it was just service with a smile. Whether you were a man, woman, or child, there was always somebody there willing just to go the extra mile, just waiting patiently to extend a helping hand, just trying to serve their fellow man.

Now, everything they did, they did very well. Now, this kind of love wasn't for sale because the love they had for you was so genuine and true. If Jesus was there, tell me what will he do? If you needed some bread, milk, and honey and you didn't have any money and you were just destitute of daily food.

Oh' Pop Holloway understood. Take what you lack, and fill your sack. Your extended credit was good for if you were in need and I did not feed, how will it profit me? It's James 2:15, if you know what I mean. To be a

Christian, you must be willing to serve. You must have an attitude for servitude and be a good servant that only God can use.

To be used by God, it's an honor to do because God doesn't hurt what he loves and certainly want to abuse you. So use me Lord in every way, I only said that to say, God uses whom he may to spread his good news, whether through service or good food. It's just some old-time tradition, with some old-time religion so that you see, it's just good enough for me."

Holy Matrimony

It must've been God's perfect will, because the day I met you my love, it's like heaven stood still. When I saw you standing there, I knew it was the end of my search. I knew I had found my wife to love, like Christ first loved the church. Just like Christ, I would give up for you all of my past life. But the only thing I ask of you, just only be my wife.

I thought this day will never come, Lord, what is a man to do? A beauty that's so young, I wonder is this fantasy true. So long I prayed for a woman that I can make my queen. I never imagined that it would be you, the angel that visits my dream.

Your body is like a love goddess so beautiful and wonderfully made, shaped by the Potter's hand with his fistful of clay, and I still can't believe what God created. With you, my love, I would be so proud to speak our wedding vows, to have and to hold forevermore and to take you in my life.

I will take you to be forever with me, my lawfully wedded wife. I looked at you with love and truth and with so much passion and pride, me as your handsome husband and you as my beautiful bride. When I look upon your gorgeous face, I see a seven-carat ring because he who finds a wife, has found a very good thing.

Now, we celebrate our wedding day. Our families have assembled to see. There she is, my bride to be looking so divine and cute, her in a long white gown and me in my long black suite. God didn't intend for me to spend my life so sad and lonely, so now I'm standing here hand in hand in holy matrimony.

Oh' Lord, now that we have gotten this far, I know you are willing and able. Thank you for your perfect love for me, and thank you for your favor. In the intimacy of our marriage, the covenant secret is revealed. Instituted by God, now the sacred bond is sealed. We consummated our love for each other, and now you've given me your best. One man, one woman, and now we are one flesh."

Just Imagine

Just imagine your life being hopeless in shame, full of disappointment, heartaches, and pain. I felt so defeated. I was lied on and cheated. I was talked about and mistreated. Just imagine having no purpose to breathe until you finally gave up and decided to conceive. Just imagine that you reached down and found a feeling that was buried deep within, something that was telling you your life wasn't going to stop. In fact, it will begin.

Just imagine sleepless nights and countless fights with oneself. But Lord, you stayed close to me, and you said you'll never leave, and I mean you never left. You've been so consistent with me in my time of need and a constant source of which comes my help. So please stay with me, Lord, because life is so hard.

I just can't even imagine life without you, God, because all my help comes from the Lord. I'm just trying to imagine how you reached down and found nothing that didn't even exist and then created something out of nothing and blew life into existence. I can imagine how you looked upon man and saw he had no blemish because you knew you had innovated something very unique into your own image.

But I imagine that you weren't through because you created one woman for one man, and now, there're two. I can imagine that the sun was shining and the skies were blue. There were white doves in heaven that were chirping, "Hallelujah." I can just imagine because they knew that God's most wonderful and magnificent creation…was you."

Kill 'Em with Kindness

Look 'em in the eyes, and just cock back your smile because a smile to your adversary will shoot 'em a mile. When they say, "You are nothing, and you won't succeed." Just say "Please" and "Thank you" and do a good deed. When they scandalize your name and criticize your fame, cut 'em up with kindness till you make 'em a shame.

When they fabricate their lies and distort the truth, strangle them with love until your enemies are through. Just like the Lord, I'm going to deal kindly with you. It's silence with no violence. That's how you kill a snake. Just give 'em Ruth 1:8. When all of hell's fury they tried to unleash, drown them with kindness until they all are deceased.

Now, let us bow our heads while they rest in peace because if the devil can kill you, better believe he will. So thank your heavenly stars that looks don't kill. That's a fact and not fiction because the devil is real. My enemies got me surrounded, but whom shall I fear? My trust is in him, and it's he that surrounds them.

So I'm going to bless the wrong with a spiritual song. That's how you break their bones with sticks and stones. I'm going to kiss and hug them to death while they're taking their last breath. So be kind to a deceiver. You might make a believer. Even God is kind to the unthankful and evil. In Luke 6:35, there's no need for riots. I'm just shopping with them wise, while I'm chopping them down to size. This is the sensational art on how to kill your enemies quite.

Hello, Heartbreak

"Hello, heartbreak" is what she say, when she looks in the mirror every day. She often kneels on her knees to pray while asking God, "Why can't I stop living this way? She can't be with the one she loves, so she loves the one that she's wit'."

She can't believe the love that got away is the love that she didn't get. So she wanted something different, something fresh and brand new. So she packs her bags with clothes and puts on her travel shoes. She wanted to see the world from a different point of view, so she chose to sail the world from an oceanside view.

Searching for the love she lost and the love she once knew. But the love she thought she found turns out to be fake. Now she's asking God, "How can I live with another mistake?" Now, she stares at the face in the mirror because it looks so familiar, then she says, "Hello, heartbreak."

Sleepless nights and countless fights, but he can care less about her sacrifice or if she's been around the world twice, so once again, she's a battered wife. Now, she's putting on makeup rouge, just to cover up her despicable bruises. It's so much hollowin' and screamin'. She can't seem to shake her demons.

They'll follow her wherever she goes, travelin' back and forth. And wherever she goes, it's the same old foes. So she prays for better days because she has a son and daughter to raise. And nothing will ever be the same. Now, she's addicted to pain. Now, her back is against the wall. Now, he realizes and apologizes and then blames it on the alcohol.

It's a trip how she embraces her abusive relationship. It's such a mean turbulent scene. Now, she's asking God to intervene. But she's really not sure what he's going to do, but she knows she's tired of feeling like yesterday's news. Now, she's all fed up. She took all she can take but takes another glance in the mirror and says, "Hello, heartbreak."

Now, she's going through rain and stormy weather, but she knows very well that her mama taught her better. Just take a little while to listen child, and don't you ever settle. And never forget that love is not jealous or even envious. And don't be confused with love and lust. Remember, God's love is a perfect love that comes from above, and don't ever equate fear with love.

And know that God is always near and a perfect love casts out all fear. Even if you're seven thousand miles away and you are oceans apart, nothing can ever separate you from the love of God. Now, she's convinced, and it all makes perfect sense. Now, she knows that she's traveled the world trying to find the love that was there all the time.

The love that was there in her times of need and would love her unconditionally. The love that doesn't care about her past mistakes and truly will love her throughout all her pain and aches. Now, there is a new face that's clearer when she looks in the mirror and says, "So long, heartbreak."

About the Author

Victor L. Brackett Jr. is the son of a Pentecostal minister. He's from Birmingham, Alabama. He's happily married and has three beautiful children. He's a devout Christian. He has been writing spiritual poetry over twenty years.

God has truly given him this incredible gift to spread his message of love, life, and relationships through spiritual poetry. He believes in his heart that this is his mission, as well as his passion to do. He always dreamed of writing spiritual novels, but he never imagined that it would ever become a reality.

His mother, who was a Pentecostal minister, as he stated, prophesied to him. She told him that one day, he would be writing books. He must confess that at times, he thought that it would never happen for him. But he stayed faithful to God's Word and continued to do what God had called him to do, which is write.

He truly wants to thank Christian Faith Publishing for making his dream a reality and fulfilling the prophecy that God intended for his life.